50 Ultimate Pasta Dishes for Home

By: Kelly Johnson

Table of Contents

- Classic Spaghetti Carbonara
- Fettuccine Alfredo
- Pesto Pasta with Pine Nuts
- Baked Ziti with Mozzarella
- Shrimp Scampi Linguine
- Cacio e Pepe
- Spaghetti Bolognese
- Creamy Tuscan Chicken Pasta
- Lasagna Bolognese
- Pasta Primavera
- Lobster Mac and Cheese
- Garlic Butter Parmesan Orzo
- Mushroom Truffle Pasta
- Penne alla Vodka
- Cajun Chicken Pasta
- Beef Stroganoff Pasta
- Spaghetti Aglio e Olio
- Four-Cheese Ravioli
- Sicilian Caponata Pasta
- Tuna Pasta with Olives
- Orecchiette with Sausage and Broccoli Rabe
- Spinach and Ricotta Stuffed Shells
- Lemon Butter Shrimp Pasta
- Chicken Pesto Penne
- Gnocchi with Brown Butter and Sage
- Roasted Red Pepper Pasta
- Seafood Marinara Pasta
- Vegan Creamy Avocado Pasta
- Sun-Dried Tomato and Basil Pasta
- Chicken Parmesan Pasta Bake
- Lemon Garlic Asparagus Pasta
- Pumpkin Alfredo Pasta
- Pasta Puttanesca
- Zucchini Noodle Pasta with Pesto
- Meatball Marinara Spaghetti

- Crab Linguine with Lemon and Chili
- Mushroom and Spinach Ravioli
- Roasted Garlic and Tomato Penne
- Beef Ragu Pappardelle
- Spaghetti with Clam Sauce
- Truffle Mac and Cheese
- Sweet Potato Gnocchi with Sage
- Chicken Marsala Pasta
- Eggplant Parmesan Pasta
- Ricotta and Spinach Cannelloni
- Chorizo and Tomato Pasta
- Lemon Ricotta Pasta with Peas
- Greek Pasta Salad with Feta
- Black Pepper and Parmesan Bucatini
- Pesto Tortellini with Sun-Dried Tomatoes

Classic Spaghetti Carbonara

Ingredients:

- 12 oz (340g) spaghetti
- 4 oz (115g) pancetta, diced
- 2 large eggs
- ½ cup (50g) grated Parmesan cheese
- 1 teaspoon black pepper
- 2 cloves garlic, minced
- Salt to taste

Instructions:

1. **Cook Spaghetti:** Boil in salted water until al dente. Reserve ½ cup pasta water.
2. **Cook Pancetta:** Sauté in a pan until crispy. Add garlic and cook for 30 seconds.
3. **Prepare Sauce:** Whisk eggs, Parmesan, and black pepper in a bowl.
4. **Combine:** Toss hot pasta with pancetta and remove from heat. Slowly mix in egg mixture, adding reserved pasta water as needed for creaminess. Serve immediately.

Fettuccine Alfredo

Ingredients:

- 12 oz (340g) fettuccine
- 1 cup (240ml) heavy cream
- ½ cup (113g) unsalted butter
- 1 cup (100g) grated Parmesan cheese
- Salt and black pepper to taste

Instructions:

1. **Cook Pasta:** Boil fettuccine in salted water until al dente.
2. **Make Sauce:** Melt butter in a pan, add cream, and simmer for 2 minutes. Stir in Parmesan cheese.
3. **Combine:** Toss pasta in the sauce, season with salt and black pepper, and serve hot.

Pesto Pasta with Pine Nuts

Ingredients:

- 12 oz (340g) pasta of choice
- 2 cups (60g) fresh basil leaves
- ¼ cup (30g) pine nuts
- ½ cup (50g) grated Parmesan cheese
- 2 cloves garlic
- ½ cup (120ml) olive oil
- Salt and black pepper to taste

Instructions:

1. **Cook Pasta:** Boil in salted water until al dente.
2. **Make Pesto:** Blend basil, pine nuts, garlic, Parmesan, and olive oil until smooth.
3. **Combine:** Toss pasta with pesto and serve immediately.

Baked Ziti with Mozzarella

Ingredients:

- 12 oz (340g) ziti pasta
- 2 cups (480ml) marinara sauce
- 1 cup (200g) ricotta cheese
- 1 cup (100g) shredded mozzarella
- ½ cup (50g) grated Parmesan cheese
- 1 teaspoon Italian seasoning

Instructions:

1. **Cook Pasta:** Boil ziti in salted water until al dente.
2. **Mix Ingredients:** Combine pasta, marinara sauce, ricotta, and Italian seasoning.
3. **Bake:** Pour into a baking dish, top with mozzarella and Parmesan, and bake at 375°F (190°C) for 20 minutes.

Shrimp Scampi Linguine

Ingredients:

- 12 oz (340g) linguine
- 1 lb (450g) shrimp, peeled and deveined
- 4 cloves garlic, minced
- ½ cup (120ml) white wine
- ¼ cup (60ml) lemon juice
- ¼ cup (60g) butter
- 2 tablespoons olive oil
- ¼ teaspoon red pepper flakes
- Salt and black pepper to taste

Instructions:

1. **Cook Pasta:** Boil linguine in salted water until al dente.
2. **Cook Shrimp:** Sauté garlic in olive oil and butter, add shrimp, and cook for 2 minutes per side.
3. **Add Sauce:** Pour in wine and lemon juice, simmer for 2 minutes. Toss with pasta and serve.

Cacio e Pepe

Ingredients:

- 12 oz (340g) spaghetti
- 1 cup (100g) grated Pecorino Romano cheese
- 1 teaspoon black pepper
- ½ cup (120ml) reserved pasta water

Instructions:

1. **Cook Pasta:** Boil in salted water until al dente. Reserve pasta water.
2. **Make Sauce:** Toast black pepper in a pan, add pasta water, and melt cheese into it.
3. **Combine:** Toss pasta with sauce and serve.

Spaghetti Bolognese

Ingredients:

- 12 oz (340g) spaghetti
- 1 lb (450g) ground beef
- 1 onion, diced
- 2 cloves garlic, minced
- 1 can (14 oz / 400g) crushed tomatoes
- ½ cup (120ml) red wine
- 1 teaspoon Italian seasoning
- Salt and black pepper to taste

Instructions:

1. **Cook Pasta:** Boil spaghetti in salted water until al dente.
2. **Make Sauce:** Brown beef in a pan, add onion and garlic, and cook until soft. Stir in tomatoes, wine, and seasoning, and simmer for 20 minutes.
3. **Combine:** Toss pasta with sauce and serve.

Creamy Tuscan Chicken Pasta

Ingredients:

- 12 oz (340g) penne pasta
- 2 chicken breasts, sliced
- 1 cup (240ml) heavy cream
- ½ cup (100g) sun-dried tomatoes, chopped
- 2 cloves garlic, minced
- 1 cup (100g) spinach
- ½ cup (50g) grated Parmesan

Instructions:

1. **Cook Pasta:** Boil penne in salted water until al dente.
2. **Cook Chicken:** Sauté in a pan until golden brown, then remove.
3. **Make Sauce:** In the same pan, cook garlic, sun-dried tomatoes, and cream. Stir in spinach and Parmesan.
4. **Combine:** Add chicken and pasta to the sauce, toss, and serve.

Lasagna Bolognese

Ingredients:

- 12 lasagna sheets
- 1 lb (450g) ground beef
- 1 onion, diced
- 2 cloves garlic, minced
- 2 cups (480ml) marinara sauce
- 1 cup (250g) ricotta cheese
- 1 cup (100g) shredded mozzarella
- ½ cup (50g) grated Parmesan

Instructions:

1. **Cook Beef:** Brown with onion and garlic. Stir in marinara sauce and simmer for 10 minutes.
2. **Assemble Layers:** Layer lasagna sheets, meat sauce, ricotta, mozzarella, and Parmesan.
3. **Bake:** Bake at 375°F (190°C) for 40 minutes.

Pasta Primavera

Ingredients:

- 12 oz (340g) pasta of choice
- 1 zucchini, sliced
- 1 bell pepper, sliced
- 1 carrot, julienned
- 1 cup (150g) cherry tomatoes, halved
- 2 cloves garlic, minced
- ½ cup (120ml) olive oil
- Salt and black pepper to taste

Instructions:

1. **Cook Pasta:** Boil in salted water until al dente.
2. **Sauté Vegetables:** Cook garlic, zucchini, bell pepper, and carrot in olive oil until tender.
3. **Combine:** Toss pasta with sautéed vegetables, cherry tomatoes, and season to taste.

Lobster Mac and Cheese

Ingredients:

- 12 oz (340g) elbow macaroni
- 2 cups (480ml) whole milk
- 1 cup (240ml) heavy cream
- 2 cups (200g) shredded sharp cheddar cheese
- 1 cup (100g) shredded Gruyère cheese
- 1 cup (150g) cooked lobster meat, chopped
- 3 tablespoons butter
- 2 tablespoons all-purpose flour
- ½ teaspoon paprika
- Salt and black pepper to taste

Instructions:

1. **Cook Pasta:** Boil macaroni in salted water until al dente.
2. **Make Cheese Sauce:** Melt butter, stir in flour, and cook for 1 minute. Gradually whisk in milk and cream, then add cheeses, paprika, salt, and pepper.
3. **Combine:** Stir in pasta and lobster, then serve warm.

Garlic Butter Parmesan Orzo

Ingredients:

- 1 cup (200g) orzo pasta
- 2 cups (480ml) chicken broth
- 2 tablespoons butter
- 2 cloves garlic, minced
- ½ cup (50g) grated Parmesan cheese
- 2 tablespoons chopped parsley

Instructions:

1. **Cook Orzo:** Sauté garlic in butter, then add orzo and toast for 1 minute.
2. **Simmer:** Pour in chicken broth, cover, and cook until liquid is absorbed.
3. **Finish:** Stir in Parmesan and parsley before serving.

Mushroom Truffle Pasta

Ingredients:

- 12 oz (340g) pasta of choice
- 2 tablespoons truffle oil
- 1 cup (150g) mushrooms, sliced
- ½ cup (120ml) heavy cream
- ½ cup (50g) grated Parmesan cheese
- Salt and black pepper to taste

Instructions:

1. **Cook Pasta:** Boil pasta in salted water until al dente.
2. **Sauté Mushrooms:** Cook mushrooms in a pan with truffle oil until tender.
3. **Make Sauce:** Add cream, Parmesan, salt, and pepper.
4. **Combine:** Toss with pasta and serve.

Penne alla Vodka

Ingredients:

- 12 oz (340g) penne pasta
- 1 cup (240ml) tomato sauce
- ½ cup (120ml) heavy cream
- ¼ cup (60ml) vodka
- 2 tablespoons olive oil
- 1 teaspoon red pepper flakes
- ½ cup (50g) grated Parmesan cheese

Instructions:

1. **Cook Pasta:** Boil penne in salted water until al dente.
2. **Prepare Sauce:** Heat olive oil, add red pepper flakes, then pour in vodka and let simmer for 2 minutes.
3. **Finish Sauce:** Stir in tomato sauce and heavy cream, then add Parmesan.
4. **Combine:** Toss pasta in sauce and serve.

Cajun Chicken Pasta

Ingredients:

- 12 oz (340g) penne pasta
- 2 chicken breasts, sliced
- 1 tablespoon Cajun seasoning
- 1 cup (240ml) heavy cream
- ½ cup (50g) grated Parmesan cheese
- 2 cloves garlic, minced
- 2 tablespoons butter

Instructions:

1. **Cook Pasta:** Boil in salted water until al dente.
2. **Cook Chicken:** Sauté chicken with Cajun seasoning until golden brown.
3. **Make Sauce:** In the same pan, melt butter, add garlic, cream, and Parmesan.
4. **Combine:** Toss pasta with sauce and chicken before serving.

Beef Stroganoff Pasta

Ingredients:

- 12 oz (340g) egg noodles
- 1 lb (450g) beef sirloin, sliced
- 1 cup (150g) mushrooms, sliced
- 1 onion, diced
- 1 cup (240ml) beef broth
- ½ cup (120ml) sour cream
- 2 tablespoons flour

Instructions:

1. **Cook Pasta:** Boil egg noodles in salted water until al dente.
2. **Cook Beef:** Sauté beef until browned, then remove from pan.
3. **Make Sauce:** Sauté onion and mushrooms, add flour, then stir in beef broth and simmer.
4. **Finish:** Return beef to the pan, stir in sour cream, and toss with pasta.

Spaghetti Aglio e Olio

Ingredients:

- 12 oz (340g) spaghetti
- 4 cloves garlic, sliced
- ¼ cup (60ml) olive oil
- ½ teaspoon red pepper flakes
- ¼ cup (25g) grated Parmesan cheese
- 2 tablespoons chopped parsley

Instructions:

1. **Cook Pasta:** Boil in salted water until al dente. Reserve some pasta water.
2. **Sauté Garlic:** Heat olive oil and cook garlic until golden.
3. **Combine:** Toss pasta with garlic oil, red pepper flakes, Parmesan, and parsley. Add pasta water if needed.

Four-Cheese Ravioli

Ingredients:

- 12 oz (340g) store-bought ravioli
- 1 cup (240ml) heavy cream
- ¼ cup (25g) grated mozzarella
- ¼ cup (25g) grated Parmesan
- ¼ cup (25g) grated Fontina
- ¼ cup (25g) grated Ricotta
- Salt and black pepper to taste

Instructions:

1. **Cook Ravioli:** Boil in salted water until tender.
2. **Make Sauce:** Heat cream, then whisk in cheeses until melted.
3. **Combine:** Toss ravioli in sauce and serve warm.

Sicilian Caponata Pasta

Ingredients:

- 12 oz (340g) pasta
- 1 eggplant, diced
- 1 bell pepper, diced
- 1 onion, chopped
- 2 cloves garlic, minced
- 1 can (14 oz / 400g) crushed tomatoes
- ¼ cup (60ml) red wine vinegar
- 2 tablespoons capers

Instructions:

1. **Cook Pasta:** Boil in salted water until al dente.
2. **Cook Vegetables:** Sauté eggplant, pepper, onion, and garlic.
3. **Make Sauce:** Stir in tomatoes, vinegar, and capers, then simmer.
4. **Combine:** Toss pasta with sauce and serve.

Tuna Pasta with Olives

Ingredients:

- 12 oz (340g) spaghetti
- 1 can (6 oz / 170g) tuna, drained
- ½ cup (75g) black olives, sliced
- 2 cloves garlic, minced
- 2 tablespoons olive oil
- ½ teaspoon red pepper flakes

Instructions:

1. **Cook Pasta:** Boil in salted water until al dente.
2. **Sauté Ingredients:** Cook garlic in olive oil, add tuna and olives.
3. **Combine:** Toss pasta with sauce, add red pepper flakes, and serve.

Orecchiette with Sausage and Broccoli Rabe

Ingredients:

- 12 oz (340g) orecchiette pasta
- ½ lb (225g) Italian sausage, crumbled
- 1 bunch broccoli rabe, chopped
- 2 cloves garlic, minced
- 2 tablespoons olive oil
- ½ teaspoon red pepper flakes

Instructions:

1. **Cook Pasta:** Boil in salted water until al dente.
2. **Cook Sausage:** Brown in a pan, then remove.
3. **Sauté Garlic & Broccoli Rabe:** Cook in the same pan with olive oil.
4. **Combine:** Return sausage, toss with pasta, and serve.

Spinach and Ricotta Stuffed Shells

Ingredients:

- 12 oz (340g) jumbo pasta shells
- 2 cups (500g) ricotta cheese
- 1 cup (100g) shredded mozzarella cheese
- ½ cup (50g) grated Parmesan cheese
- 2 cups (480ml) marinara sauce
- 2 cups (60g) fresh spinach, chopped
- 1 egg
- 1 teaspoon Italian seasoning
- Salt and black pepper to taste

Instructions:

1. **Cook Pasta:** Boil shells in salted water until al dente. Drain and set aside.
2. **Prepare Filling:** Mix ricotta, mozzarella, Parmesan, spinach, egg, Italian seasoning, salt, and pepper.
3. **Assemble & Bake:** Fill shells with ricotta mixture, place in a baking dish with marinara sauce, and bake at 375°F (190°C) for 25 minutes.

Lemon Butter Shrimp Pasta

Ingredients:

- 12 oz (340g) linguine
- 1 lb (450g) shrimp, peeled and deveined
- 4 tablespoons butter
- 2 cloves garlic, minced
- ½ cup (120ml) white wine
- ¼ cup (60ml) lemon juice
- ½ teaspoon red pepper flakes
- ¼ cup (25g) grated Parmesan cheese

Instructions:

1. **Cook Pasta:** Boil linguine in salted water until al dente.
2. **Cook Shrimp:** Sauté shrimp in butter for 2 minutes per side, then remove.
3. **Make Sauce:** Cook garlic, add wine and lemon juice, and simmer for 2 minutes.
4. **Combine:** Toss pasta and shrimp in sauce, sprinkle with Parmesan, and serve.

Chicken Pesto Penne

Ingredients:

- 12 oz (340g) penne pasta
- 2 chicken breasts, diced
- ½ cup (120g) pesto sauce
- ½ cup (100g) cherry tomatoes, halved
- ½ cup (50g) grated Parmesan cheese
- 2 tablespoons olive oil

Instructions:

1. **Cook Pasta:** Boil penne in salted water until al dente.
2. **Cook Chicken:** Sauté chicken in olive oil until golden brown.
3. **Combine:** Toss pasta with pesto, chicken, tomatoes, and Parmesan.

Gnocchi with Brown Butter and Sage

Ingredients:

- 12 oz (340g) potato gnocchi
- 4 tablespoons unsalted butter
- 6 fresh sage leaves
- ½ cup (50g) grated Parmesan cheese

Instructions:

1. **Cook Gnocchi:** Boil in salted water until they float to the top.
2. **Make Sauce:** Melt butter, add sage leaves, and cook until fragrant.
3. **Combine:** Toss gnocchi in brown butter sauce and top with Parmesan.

Roasted Red Pepper Pasta

Ingredients:

- 12 oz (340g) pasta of choice
- 2 roasted red peppers, blended
- ½ cup (120ml) heavy cream
- 2 cloves garlic, minced
- ½ teaspoon red pepper flakes
- ½ cup (50g) grated Parmesan cheese

Instructions:

1. **Cook Pasta:** Boil in salted water until al dente.
2. **Make Sauce:** Sauté garlic, add blended peppers, red pepper flakes, and cream. Simmer for 5 minutes.
3. **Combine:** Toss pasta in sauce and top with Parmesan.

Seafood Marinara Pasta

Ingredients:

- 12 oz (340g) spaghetti
- ½ lb (225g) shrimp
- ½ lb (225g) mussels
- 2 cups (480ml) marinara sauce
- 2 cloves garlic, minced
- ½ cup (120ml) white wine
- 2 tablespoons olive oil

Instructions:

1. **Cook Pasta:** Boil spaghetti in salted water until al dente.
2. **Cook Seafood:** Sauté garlic in olive oil, add shrimp and mussels, then pour in wine and simmer.
3. **Make Sauce:** Stir in marinara sauce, let simmer, then toss with pasta.

Vegan Creamy Avocado Pasta

Ingredients:

- 12 oz (340g) spaghetti
- 2 ripe avocados
- 1 cup (240ml) plant-based milk
- 2 tablespoons lemon juice
- 2 cloves garlic
- ¼ cup (25g) nutritional yeast
- Salt and black pepper to taste

Instructions:

1. **Cook Pasta:** Boil spaghetti in salted water until al dente.
2. **Blend Sauce:** Mix avocados, milk, lemon juice, garlic, and nutritional yeast until smooth.
3. **Combine:** Toss pasta with sauce and serve.

Sun-Dried Tomato and Basil Pasta

Ingredients:

- 12 oz (340g) penne pasta
- ½ cup (100g) sun-dried tomatoes, chopped
- 2 cloves garlic, minced
- ½ cup (120ml) heavy cream
- ½ cup (50g) grated Parmesan cheese
- ½ cup (10g) fresh basil, chopped

Instructions:

1. **Cook Pasta:** Boil in salted water until al dente.
2. **Make Sauce:** Sauté garlic, add sun-dried tomatoes and cream, and simmer.
3. **Combine:** Toss pasta with sauce, Parmesan, and basil.

Chicken Parmesan Pasta Bake

Ingredients:

- 12 oz (340g) penne pasta
- 2 chicken breasts, diced
- 2 cups (480ml) marinara sauce
- 1 cup (100g) shredded mozzarella cheese
- ½ cup (50g) grated Parmesan cheese
- 1 teaspoon Italian seasoning

Instructions:

1. **Cook Pasta:** Boil in salted water until al dente.
2. **Cook Chicken:** Sauté chicken until golden brown.
3. **Assemble & Bake:** Mix pasta, marinara, and chicken in a dish. Top with cheeses and bake at 375°F (190°C) for 25 minutes.

Lemon Garlic Asparagus Pasta

Ingredients:

- 12 oz (340g) pasta
- 1 bunch asparagus, chopped
- 2 cloves garlic, minced
- 2 tablespoons olive oil
- ½ cup (50g) grated Parmesan cheese
- ¼ cup (60ml) lemon juice

Instructions:

1. **Cook Pasta:** Boil in salted water until al dente.
2. **Sauté Asparagus:** Cook asparagus and garlic in olive oil for 3 minutes.
3. **Combine:** Toss pasta with asparagus, lemon juice, and Parmesan.

Pumpkin Alfredo Pasta

Ingredients:

- 12 oz (340g) fettuccine
- 1 cup (240ml) pumpkin purée
- 1 cup (240ml) heavy cream
- ½ cup (50g) grated Parmesan cheese
- 2 cloves garlic, minced
- 2 tablespoons butter

Instructions:

1. **Cook Pasta:** Boil in salted water until al dente.
2. **Make Sauce:** Sauté garlic in butter, add pumpkin purée and cream, and simmer for 5 minutes.
3. **Combine:** Toss pasta with sauce, stir in Parmesan, and serve.

Pasta Puttanesca

Ingredients:

- 12 oz (340g) spaghetti
- 2 tablespoons olive oil
- 3 cloves garlic, minced
- 1 teaspoon red pepper flakes
- 1 can (14 oz / 400g) crushed tomatoes
- ½ cup (75g) black olives, sliced
- 2 tablespoons capers
- 4 anchovy fillets, chopped
- ½ teaspoon dried oregano
- ¼ cup (10g) fresh parsley, chopped

Instructions:

1. **Cook Pasta:** Boil spaghetti in salted water until al dente.
2. **Make Sauce:** Heat olive oil, sauté garlic and red pepper flakes. Stir in tomatoes, olives, capers, anchovies, and oregano. Simmer for 10 minutes.
3. **Combine:** Toss pasta with sauce and garnish with parsley.

Zucchini Noodle Pasta with Pesto

Ingredients:

- 4 medium zucchini, spiralized
- ½ cup (120g) pesto sauce
- ¼ cup (25g) grated Parmesan cheese
- 2 tablespoons olive oil
- 1 teaspoon lemon juice
- ½ teaspoon black pepper

Instructions:

1. **Sauté Zucchini:** Cook zucchini noodles in olive oil for 2 minutes.
2. **Mix with Sauce:** Remove from heat and toss with pesto, lemon juice, and black pepper.
3. **Serve:** Sprinkle with Parmesan before serving.

Meatball Marinara Spaghetti

Ingredients:

- 12 oz (340g) spaghetti
- 1 lb (450g) ground beef
- ½ cup (50g) breadcrumbs
- 1 egg
- 2 cloves garlic, minced
- 2 cups (480ml) marinara sauce
- ½ cup (50g) grated Parmesan cheese
- 1 teaspoon Italian seasoning

Instructions:

1. **Make Meatballs:** Mix beef, breadcrumbs, egg, garlic, Parmesan, and seasoning. Form into balls and bake at 375°F (190°C) for 15 minutes.
2. **Cook Pasta:** Boil spaghetti in salted water until al dente.
3. **Simmer Sauce:** Heat marinara sauce, add cooked meatballs, and let simmer for 5 minutes.
4. **Combine:** Toss pasta with sauce and serve.

Crab Linguine with Lemon and Chili

Ingredients:

- 12 oz (340g) linguine
- 1 cup (150g) fresh crab meat
- 2 tablespoons olive oil
- 2 cloves garlic, minced
- ½ teaspoon red pepper flakes
- ¼ cup (60ml) lemon juice
- ¼ cup (10g) fresh parsley, chopped

Instructions:

1. **Cook Pasta:** Boil linguine in salted water until al dente.
2. **Prepare Sauce:** Heat olive oil, sauté garlic and red pepper flakes, then stir in crab meat.
3. **Combine:** Toss pasta with sauce, lemon juice, and parsley.

Mushroom and Spinach Ravioli

Ingredients:

- 12 oz (340g) store-bought ravioli
- 2 tablespoons butter
- 1 cup (150g) mushrooms, sliced
- 2 cups (60g) fresh spinach
- ½ cup (120ml) heavy cream
- ½ cup (50g) grated Parmesan cheese

Instructions:

1. **Cook Ravioli:** Boil in salted water until tender.
2. **Sauté Mushrooms:** Cook mushrooms in butter until soft, then add spinach.
3. **Make Sauce:** Stir in cream and Parmesan, then toss with ravioli.

Roasted Garlic and Tomato Penne

Ingredients:

- 12 oz (340g) penne pasta
- 1 pint (300g) cherry tomatoes, halved
- 1 head garlic, roasted
- 2 tablespoons olive oil
- ½ teaspoon red pepper flakes
- ½ cup (50g) grated Parmesan cheese

Instructions:

1. **Roast Garlic & Tomatoes:** Place tomatoes and garlic in the oven at 375°F (190°C) for 20 minutes.
2. **Cook Pasta:** Boil penne in salted water until al dente.
3. **Combine:** Toss pasta with roasted garlic (mashed), tomatoes, olive oil, red pepper flakes, and Parmesan.

Beef Ragu Pappardelle

Ingredients:

- 12 oz (340g) pappardelle pasta
- 1 lb (450g) beef chuck, shredded
- 1 onion, diced
- 2 cloves garlic, minced
- 1 can (14 oz / 400g) crushed tomatoes
- ½ cup (120ml) red wine
- 1 teaspoon dried thyme

Instructions:

1. **Cook Beef:** Sear beef in a pan, then remove.
2. **Make Sauce:** Sauté onion and garlic, add tomatoes, wine, and thyme, then return beef and simmer for 1 hour.
3. **Cook Pasta:** Boil pappardelle in salted water until al dente.
4. **Combine:** Toss pasta with ragu and serve.

Spaghetti with Clam Sauce

Ingredients:

- 12 oz (340g) spaghetti
- 1 lb (450g) fresh clams
- 2 tablespoons olive oil
- 2 cloves garlic, minced
- ½ cup (120ml) white wine
- ¼ teaspoon red pepper flakes
- ¼ cup (10g) fresh parsley, chopped

Instructions:

1. **Cook Pasta:** Boil spaghetti in salted water until al dente.
2. **Cook Clams:** Sauté garlic and red pepper flakes in olive oil, then add clams and wine. Cover and cook until clams open.
3. **Combine:** Toss pasta with clams and parsley before serving.

Truffle Mac and Cheese

Ingredients:

- 12 oz (340g) elbow macaroni
- 2 cups (480ml) whole milk
- 1 cup (100g) shredded Gruyère cheese
- 1 cup (100g) shredded white cheddar cheese
- 2 tablespoons truffle oil
- 2 tablespoons butter
- 2 tablespoons flour

Instructions:

1. **Cook Pasta:** Boil macaroni in salted water until al dente.
2. **Make Sauce:** Melt butter, whisk in flour, then gradually add milk. Stir in cheeses and truffle oil.
3. **Combine:** Toss pasta in sauce and serve warm.

Sweet Potato Gnocchi with Sage

Ingredients:

- 2 medium sweet potatoes, mashed
- 1 cup (120g) all-purpose flour
- 1 egg yolk
- ½ teaspoon salt
- 4 tablespoons butter
- 6 fresh sage leaves

Instructions:

1. **Make Gnocchi:** Mix sweet potato, flour, egg yolk, and salt to form dough. Roll into ropes, cut into bite-sized pieces, and boil until they float.
2. **Brown Butter Sauce:** Melt butter in a pan, add sage leaves, and cook until butter browns.
3. **Combine:** Toss gnocchi in sauce and serve warm.

Chicken Marsala Pasta

Ingredients:

- 12 oz (340g) fettuccine or penne
- 2 chicken breasts, sliced
- 1 cup (240ml) Marsala wine
- 1 cup (240ml) chicken broth
- 1 cup (150g) mushrooms, sliced
- ½ cup (120ml) heavy cream
- 2 cloves garlic, minced
- ½ teaspoon black pepper
- 2 tablespoons olive oil
- ½ cup (50g) grated Parmesan cheese

Instructions:

1. **Cook Pasta:** Boil pasta in salted water until al dente.
2. **Cook Chicken:** Sauté chicken in olive oil until golden, then remove.
3. **Make Sauce:** Sauté garlic and mushrooms, add Marsala wine and chicken broth, and simmer. Stir in heavy cream and Parmesan.
4. **Combine:** Toss pasta and chicken in sauce before serving.

Eggplant Parmesan Pasta

Ingredients:

- 12 oz (340g) rigatoni or penne
- 1 medium eggplant, diced
- 2 cups (480ml) marinara sauce
- ½ cup (50g) grated Parmesan cheese
- 1 cup (100g) shredded mozzarella
- 2 tablespoons olive oil
- 1 teaspoon Italian seasoning

Instructions:

1. **Cook Pasta:** Boil in salted water until al dente.
2. **Cook Eggplant:** Sauté diced eggplant in olive oil until tender.
3. **Make Sauce:** Stir in marinara sauce and Italian seasoning.
4. **Combine:** Toss pasta with sauce, top with mozzarella and Parmesan, and bake at 375°F (190°C) for 15 minutes.

Ricotta and Spinach Cannelloni

Ingredients:

- 12 cannelloni pasta tubes
- 2 cups (500g) ricotta cheese
- 1 cup (60g) fresh spinach, chopped
- 1 egg
- 1 cup (100g) shredded mozzarella
- ½ cup (50g) grated Parmesan
- 2 cups (480ml) marinara sauce

Instructions:

1. **Prepare Filling:** Mix ricotta, spinach, egg, mozzarella, and Parmesan.
2. **Fill Cannelloni:** Stuff each tube with ricotta mixture.
3. **Bake:** Place in a baking dish with marinara sauce, cover, and bake at 375°F (190°C) for 30 minutes.

Chorizo and Tomato Pasta

Ingredients:

- 12 oz (340g) penne or rigatoni
- ½ lb (225g) chorizo, sliced
- 1 can (14 oz / 400g) diced tomatoes
- 2 cloves garlic, minced
- 1 teaspoon smoked paprika
- ½ teaspoon red pepper flakes
- 2 tablespoons olive oil
- ½ cup (50g) grated Parmesan cheese

Instructions:

1. **Cook Pasta:** Boil in salted water until al dente.
2. **Cook Chorizo:** Sauté chorizo until crispy, then remove.
3. **Make Sauce:** Sauté garlic, add tomatoes, paprika, and red pepper flakes, and simmer.
4. **Combine:** Toss pasta with sauce and chorizo, then top with Parmesan.

Lemon Ricotta Pasta with Peas

Ingredients:

- 12 oz (340g) spaghetti or linguine
- 1 cup (250g) ricotta cheese
- 1 cup (150g) peas
- ¼ cup (60ml) lemon juice
- 1 teaspoon lemon zest
- 2 tablespoons olive oil
- ½ cup (50g) grated Parmesan

Instructions:

1. **Cook Pasta:** Boil in salted water until al dente. Add peas in the last 2 minutes.
2. **Prepare Sauce:** Mix ricotta, lemon juice, zest, and olive oil.
3. **Combine:** Toss pasta with sauce and serve with Parmesan.

Greek Pasta Salad with Feta

Ingredients:

- 12 oz (340g) rotini or penne pasta
- 1 cup (150g) cherry tomatoes, halved
- ½ cup (75g) black olives, sliced
- ½ cup (75g) cucumber, diced
- ½ cup (75g) red onion, diced
- ½ cup (100g) feta cheese, crumbled
- ¼ cup (60ml) olive oil
- 2 tablespoons red wine vinegar
- 1 teaspoon dried oregano

Instructions:

1. **Cook Pasta:** Boil in salted water, then drain and cool.
2. **Make Dressing:** Mix olive oil, vinegar, and oregano.
3. **Combine:** Toss pasta with veggies, feta, and dressing.

Black Pepper and Parmesan Bucatini

Ingredients:

- 12 oz (340g) bucatini pasta
- 1 cup (100g) grated Parmesan cheese
- 1 tablespoon black pepper, freshly cracked
- ½ cup (120ml) reserved pasta water
- 2 tablespoons butter

Instructions:

1. **Cook Pasta:** Boil in salted water until al dente. Reserve some pasta water.
2. **Make Sauce:** Melt butter in a pan, add black pepper, and toast for 30 seconds.
3. **Combine:** Toss pasta with butter, Parmesan, and pasta water for creaminess.

Pesto Tortellini with Sun-Dried Tomatoes

Ingredients:

- 12 oz (340g) cheese tortellini
- ½ cup (120g) pesto sauce
- ½ cup (75g) sun-dried tomatoes, chopped
- ¼ cup (25g) grated Parmesan
- 2 tablespoons olive oil

Instructions:

1. **Cook Tortellini:** Boil in salted water until tender.
2. **Prepare Sauce:** Heat pesto and sun-dried tomatoes in olive oil.
3. **Combine:** Toss tortellini in sauce and serve with Parmesan.